D0184628

For Katy Thompson
W.M.

For Fritz
P.B.

First published 1984 by
Walker Books Ltd,
17-19 Hanway House,
Hanway Place, London W1P 9DL

Text © 1984 William Mayne
Illustrations © 1984 Patrick Benson

Colour separation by
Keene Engraving Ltd, London

First printed 1984
Printed and bound in Italy by L.E.G.O., Vicenza.

British Library Cataloguing in Publication Data
Mayne, William
The green book of Hob stories.
I. Title II. Benson, Patrick
823'.914[J] PZ7

ISBN 0-7445-0121-0

THE GREEN BOOK OF
HOB
STORIES

WILLIAM MAYNE

ILLUSTRATED BY PATRICK BENSON

WALKER BOOKS
LONDON

HOB AND THE STRANGE BABY

Who rocks Baby's cradle when no one is in the room?

'It's Hob,' says Baby, but even Hob does not understand his words.

'It's Hob,' says Budgie, but even Budgie does not understand her words.

'It's Hob,' say Boy and Girl, but no one believes it.

'Hob does,' says Hob. 'Hob likes Baby. I wonder why, because it isn't any use. No better than Budgie.' Budgie scowls.

Hob rocks the cradle. Baby sings.

Hob gets his reward by the fireside each night, and hopes he never is given clothes. He says, 'Never give him leather or thread, Or into the weather he will tread.'

Baby does not always sing.

'I hope he's well,' says Hob.

'Perhaps his teeth are growing,' says Mrs.

'Baby doesn't need teeth,' says Hob, and has a look. He opens Baby's mouth.

'His teeth are big,' says Hob, taking his fingers away. He rocks the cradle. Baby snores.

'Baby is a little strange,' says Girl. 'Not himself.'

'He's growing long,' says Mrs. 'He's not quite so fat.'

'He is still bald,' says Boy.

'That's how he's born,' says Mrs.

'He's eating quite a lot,' says Mr. 'Day and night, night and day.'

Hob has another look. Baby has a look at him.

'Baby looks too hard at Hob,' says Hob. 'Maybe Hob looked too hard at him.'

Now Baby does not sing at all. Baby complains. He shrieks when Budgie sings.

'That's sensible,' says Hob. 'But strange.' He looks at Baby's feet. They are long and skinny, leathery and brown, and rather worn.

'Hob wonders,' says Hob. 'Hob does.'

That night Hob is sure he sees smoke rising from the cradle. He creeps across and there is Baby smoking Hob's best pipe, puff, puff.

'This is a Changeling,' says Hob. 'I'll send it back and get the proper baby. Now, what can do the trick?'

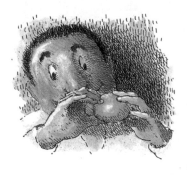

He finds his nightly gift. It is an egg. 'Hob loves an egg,' he says, 'and tonight most of all.'

First he breaks the egg and eats the yolk and white. Then he draws the fire up and makes it warm. He says out loud, for Changeling to hear, 'We'll have a pot of tea. Would you like that?'

Changeling pretends to be Baby. He does not want to be found out. But Hob knows how to send Changeling home.

Hob puts water in the egg shells and stands them on the fire. He stands the big teapot in the hearth.

'In a minute,' says Hob, 'there'll be plenty for all.'

'Nonsense,' says the Changeling. 'In all my long life I never saw tea made in egg shells.'

'Up you get,' says Hob. 'You have been found out.' And the Changeling jumps from the cradle and goes up the chimney, taking Hob's best pipe with him. A moment later Baby knocks at the door. Hob brings him in and rocks his cradle. Baby sings.

'That's that,' says Hob. 'Hob knows a thing or two.'

HOB AND MUMP

Boy and Girl know that Hob lives underneath the stairs. Mr says, 'Nonsense.' Mrs says, 'What lovely fun.' But Boy and Girl know that if they put a finger in a spyhole in the wood a little hand takes hold of it and gives a tiny squeeze.

'That's Hob,' they say. 'It's him.'

'It's Hob,' says Hob. 'It's me.'

All day he sleeps. At night he comes out and sees to things about the house and looks for his reward. Tonight he gets a buttered crust of bread. He bites it but it is hard to swallow. 'They do their best for Hob,' says Hob. He wonders why he cannot swallow simple crust.

The house is much too quiet. The clock ticks, the fire sleeps, the tap drips, the wind drives by. But it is much too quiet. Hob listens to it.

Baby is fast asleep. Budgie is not saying anything.

'That's not like Budgie,' says Hob.

Budgie is standing on her perch. She is not eating, she is not playing, she does not ring her bell.

'Too quiet for Hob,' says Hob. 'And Baby is too hot. I think there's something about.'

And roundabout Hob looks.

'Hob thinks Baby is too plump,' he says.

Budgie cannot put her head underneath her wing. A Budgie tear drops from her eye.

Hob looks. Hob finds. Hob grabs.

Hob holds a roundish, softish thing that rolls about the room. It has no face but all the same it scowls at him, and slides out from his hand. Hob takes the fireguard and traps it against the wall.

'What are you?' he asks. 'Hob wants to know. Tell Hob.'

'I'm Mump,' says roundish, softish thing. 'I talked to Baby and to Budgie and gave them mumps. Now I have to go upstairs and leave my presents there. So let me go.'

'Not yet,' says Hob. He keeps Mump prisoner while he thinks. And after he has thought he remembers what to do. He goes outside, and by the waterside he searches until he finds a certain smooth, washed stone, with a hole self-bored from front to back. Hob looks through and sees a distant star. 'Hob's found it,' he says, and hurries back.

He shows the stone to Mump. 'You will have to go,' says Hob. 'Before you go, take your present back from Baby.'

'Yes,' says Mump. He has to, with a stone like that. He does it. He has to go or be for ever in that stone. On the way he takes the present back from Baby. Hob hangs the stone in the doorway. Mump has to keep away. He cannot crawl through the stone. He has to stay out.

'Good,' says Hob. 'But my face aches.'

'And so does mine,' says Budgie. And Hob is sorry. He forgot poor Budgie. He goes up to her cage, and there he kindly chews birdseed soft for her.

Baby wakes up well, without a single mump.

HOB AND THE TEMPER

Hob lies in his cosy place underneath the stairs.

He hears Mr say to a visitor, 'This is Mrs, here are Boy and Girl and Baby. And in there is Hob, who is imaginary.'

Hob puts out his head. 'I'm not,' he says. No one  hears him. 'I wish Hob was more real,' he says.

'Told you so,' laughs Budgie. 'Hob isn't really there.'

Hob scowls, feeling cross. He goes to sleep again. He wakes up feeling sad. Something is not right. He hears Boy and Girl quarrelling at tea about the last tea-cake, and Baby cries, and someone gets a slap.

'Hob can tell,' says Hob. 'Bad times have come. Today they will give me the last present.' They give him something every night. He thinks it will be things to wear, and if it is he will have to leave.

'It happens to Hob,' he says. He stamps about the room. He slams the door of his cupboard.

He trips over something in the corner of the room.

'Mind how you go, Hob,' growls Budgie.

'What has tripped Hob?' says Hob. 'If that's the best they can do for me I'll be glad to go.'

'Temper, temper,' says Budgie.

And Hob understands his bad feelings.

'I'm not cross,' he says. 'Hob is never angry. Hob is calm. But someone's temper has been lost and left lying on the floor.'

'You leave me alone,' says Temper, in a horrible way. 'Or you'll be sorry, sorry, sorry.'

Hob steps back. It is a bad temper he has found. He must be careful.

'Steady, Hob,' he says. 'Hob, think.'

Hob thinks. He knows he must get rid of Temper. But the way to do it is quite hard for him.

'Budgie,' he says, 'Hob can't do it all alone.'

'I can't do it at all,' says Budgie. 'Get rid of it. If it comes near me my feathers will fall out.'

'We have to count backwards,' says Hob. 'From five and twenty, like blackbirds in a pie. I can't count all alone. You start, feather duster, with the biggest number.'

'Which is it?' says Budgie.

'Twenty five,' says Hob. 'I think.'

Budgie says, 'Twenty five.' Hob works it out and says, 'Twenty four.' He wakes Budgie, and she says, 'Twenty three.'

Temper begins to move towards the door. Hob and Budgie go on counting. They must not get it wrong. 'Eighteen, seventeen,' they say.

Temper stands in the porch. 'Eight, seven,' say Hob and Budgie.

Temper gets to the garden gate. 'Three, two, one,' say Hob and Budgie. 'Zero.'

'Lift-off,' says Temper, and goes stamping down the road.

'Thank you, Budgie,' says Hob. He takes his reward, the buttery tea-cake Boy and Girl fought over. He gives Budgie currants from it.

'One,' says Budgie. 'Two,' says Hob. 'Three,' says the clock.

HOB AND THE COUGH

'Poor Hob,' the children say, 'he can't be well.'
'We heard him cough,' say Girl and Boy.
'Nonsense,' says Mr, 'there's no such thing as Hob.'
'Let them have their fun,' says Mrs.

Hob is in his cupboard underneath the stairs. He hears them all. 'Hob did not cough,' he says. 'There's something going about, that's all.'

At night he comes out to look. Budgie sings.

'Quiet please, Hob's listening,' says Hob.

'Listening to me,' says Budgie, and sings a little trill.

'Hush,' says Hob. 'Listen. Did you hear that?'

There was a little trill from someone else, a little song.

'Something singing back,' says Budgie, 'because I sing so well.' And then she sings a dreadful note, like rusty iron wire.

From the fireside there comes a croaking tune, half song, half splutter.

'That's Cough,' says Hob. 'Hob doesn't know he's there until he gets in someone's song.'

'Gurr,' sings Budgie, swinging upside down to cough.

'Well, hang in there,' says Hob. 'Hob will look by the fireside.'

By the fireside a little cricket sits. He tries to sing, but every time he does the Cough starts with him.

'Saw, saw, saw,' goes Cricket.

'Hack, hack, hack,' goes Cough.

'Think, think, think,' goes Hob. Hob thinks.

'When they come down in the morning,' says Cough, 'I'll jump on Mr, Mrs, Boy, Girl, and Baby. All of them.'

Hob walks about thinking.
He grows tired of thinking.
Budgie goes, 'Hisk, hisk, hisk.'
Cricket goes, 'Husk, husk, husk.'
Hob gives up. He does not know what to do.

Hob goes to see what present has been left for him tonight. He thinks, 'If it is clothes I'll go. If I can't get rid of a simple cough I'm not fit to stay.'

In the bowl where gifts are put he finds a little bottle and a tiny spoon. In the bottle there is something black and sticky, sweet and strong. Hob knows what it is. How kind the people are to him.

It is cough syrup, cough cure. Hob takes the bottle first to Cricket.

'Open wide,' he says, and Cricket swallows down. Out jumps Cough.

'Open wide,' says Hob to Budgie. Budgie opens wide and swallows down. Cough jumps out.

'Open wide,' says Hob. Cough opens wide the door, and goes out and right away. 'That's cured that,' says Hob, and drinks a drop himself, in case.

HOB AND THE STORM

Mr takes a family photograph. The camera makes a bright light at them.

Mrs smiles and hopes her hair is tidy.

Boy frowns a bit and hopes he is printed grown up.

Girl has her tongue out, trying to lick her chin.

Baby looks cross-eyed but happy.

Mr looks at the picture when it comes back.

'It's spoilt,' he says. 'The light got in.'

Hob, in his cupboard underneath the stairs, thinks something different.

'It's Hob,' says Boy. 'Of course.'

'He's part of the family,' says Girl.

'Nonsense,' says Mr. 'The camera cannot lie. It must be broken.'

The children know it is Hob, their friend. They put the picture up for him to see.

Hob looks. 'Dear me,' he says, 'I've nothing on. Hob only dresses when he goes away.'

'All nonsense,' says Mr.

Mrs puts her thumb over that part of the picture.

Hob gets up at night and goes about the house.

'Smile please,' he says to Budgie. Budgie hides her face, all shy. She has been frightened by her own shadow when the camera winked.

Hob can't be seen in day or dark, but only in between, dawn and dusk or moonlight.

Budgie can see him now. And then a bright light comes and she can't. She sees her shadow on the wall. She thinks it is a hawk. She falls into her seed box. The shadow goes in with her.

'What was that?' says Hob. 'Another photograph?' And the bright light comes again.

The light comes sparkling at the window. It comes in and sits on the knives and spoons, and twinkles all round the room.

'Perhaps they are making a film and I'm the star,' says Budgie.

'That would be a horror film,' says Hob. 'No. Lightning has come in, that's all.'

Lightning flashes round the fire. Lightning crackles round the clock. Lightning makes the kettle boil. Lightning laughs. 'I've got away,' he says. And he makes Budgie's cage all prickly.

'This is wild, naughty lightning,' says Hob. 'And it is inside the house. I'm off,' and he goes to the door.

Lightning sits on the doorknob. Hob touches it. His hair stands on end. His teeth feel loose.

He opens the door, but he does not dare go out. Something big is there. Something is walking very large and heavy. Something monstrous in the garden is treading in the trees.

Lightning has had enough of playing on its own.

'Mother,' it shouts, 'Mother Thunder,' and goes like lightning to the big thing outside, Mother Thunder.

'Thank you,' says Mother Thunder, very rumbly. And Hob goes in. He climbs up with Budgie and they both tidy their feathers and their hair in her mirror, in the dark. Outside Mother Thunder rolls away and little Lightning sparkles in her arms.